never lose *heart*

hope for the journey

CONNIE SMITH

Never Lose Heart: Hope for the Journey

First Edition: November 2014

ISBN: 978-0-9906651-0-6

Library of Congress Control Number: 2014915247

1. Inspiration 2. Hope 3. Encouragement 4. Love 5. Comfort 6. Spirituality
I. Smith, Connie II. Never Lose Heart

Never Lose Heart may be purchased at special quantity discounts for sales promotions, premiums, corporate programs, gifts, and fundraising. For pricing information or to have Connie speak at your event, call 615-496-7006 or send an email to connie@neverloseheart.com.

Editor: Dave Carew
Layout/Design: Cheryl Casey
Publishing Consultant: Mel Cohen of Inspired Authors Press LLC
Headshot Photographer: Todd Adams Photography
Publisher: Never Lose Heart LLC

Printed in China.

www.neverloseheart.com
www.facebook.com/neverloseheartbook

Therefore we do not lose heart.

Though outwardly we are wasting away,

yet inwardly we are being renewed day by day.

2 Corinthians 4:16 (NIV)

For my mom, Billie Ann Smith,
who is a true reflection of God's love
and the greatest inspiration in my life.

acknowledgments

Thank you to my dad, Lee Smith, for believing in me and supporting me in this endeavor; to my sister, Lily Smith, for walking with me on the journey that led to the inspiration for this project; to my aunts, Bonnie Gloth and Connie Weresuk, and my dad's wife, Marilyn, for spurring me on with their enthusiasm and encouragement. And heartfelt acknowledgments to my brother, Marshall Smith, his wife, Tara, and my niece and nephew, Cali and Mac.

I am grateful for so many incredibly supportive and talented friends who have stood by me, encouraged me, prayed for me, helped me navigate the publishing world, steered me toward great resources, and given me solid input on this project. Special thanks to each of the following: Todd Adams, Amy Biter, H. Jackson Brown, Jr., Jennifer Callais, Dave Carew, Cheryl Casey, Joseph Chargois, Cindy Comperry, Kellie Conn, Pamela Daugherty, Deby Dearman, Anna Floit, Monna and Wallace Journey, Amy Kelly, Dave Killean, Mary Evelyn Kimbro, Fran Rajotte, Ken Rajotte, Michelle Reeves,

Peggy Schaefer, Susan Schumacher, Tommy Stewart, Jenny Stock, Amy Stokes, Zee Stokes, Lynn Tootle, Rob Tyree, Tim Weaver, Regan Ziegler, and everyone in my community group.

Most importantly, thank you to God, the greatest love of all, for every photo and every message in this book. *Never Lose Heart* was inspired by His love and is for His glory. May His unfailing love be known to all.

preface

Most of us have probably heard the words, "God loves you." With all of life's hardships and questions without answers, it can be difficult to believe these words in our heads, let alone in our hearts. At certain times I have asked myself, "Does God even exist?" If so, where is He and why don't I feel connected to Him? Is He disappointed in me? Up until a few years ago, I lived with the notion that if I could just get my act together and do all the right things, God would be pleased with me and start to work in my life. However, the harder I tried, the greater I failed, and the more exhausted I became.

It wasn't until I quit striving to measure up—and began to bring my true self before God with all my failures, frustrations, disappointments, hurts, and struggles—that my life started to change. As I learned to simply "be" with Him, I began to see His love in a unique way—through random hearts. I started noticing them in unexpected places in my everyday life, while walking to my car, jogging around the neighborhood, hiking in the park, running errands, doing routine tasks at home, and, most commonly, talking to God on long walks.

The more hearts I encountered, the more significant they became in my life—a confirmation of God's presence and His relentless, unconditional love. As this revelation sank deep into my heart, I began to understand the true meaning of God's grace as I had never known it before. Our brokenness and shortcomings will never stand in the way of God's love for us. It's in His love that we find true freedom and restoration. It's in His love that we find healing. It's in His love that we find power to overcome darkness. It's in His love that we find hope.

No one is exempt from hardships in this life, but God is faithful and promises to be with us no matter what, even in the midst of our failures. His unfailing love has always been there, ready to be found—if we choose to open our hearts and see it. I hope this book will encourage you to keep running the race set before you and to never lose heart. Romans 8:38-39

introduction

The purpose of this book lies in the story of the random hearts and the message within each photo – not the photography itself. I certainly do not claim to be a professional photographer. With a few exceptions, the hearts were snapped with my iPhone 4S, unaltered and just as I found them.

When you face uncertainty and
doubt in the desert of life,

I am here…

For love whispers truth
in subtle and gentle ways.

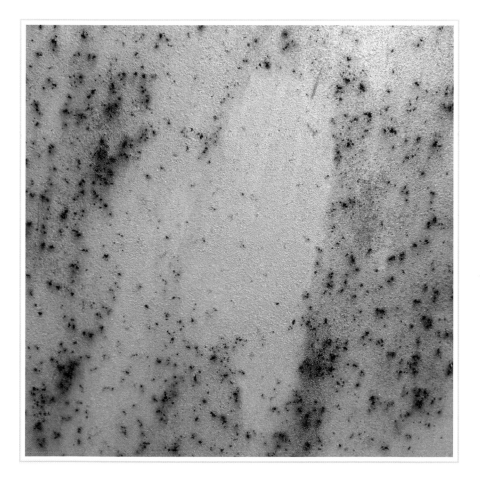

When you wander aimlessly
and miss the mark,

I am here…

For love stands strong and firm.

When you stumble over
obstacles in the road,

I am here...

For love gives the chance
for new beginnings.

When you feel yourself
slipping into the shadows,

I am here...

For love rushes near
with an outstretched hand.

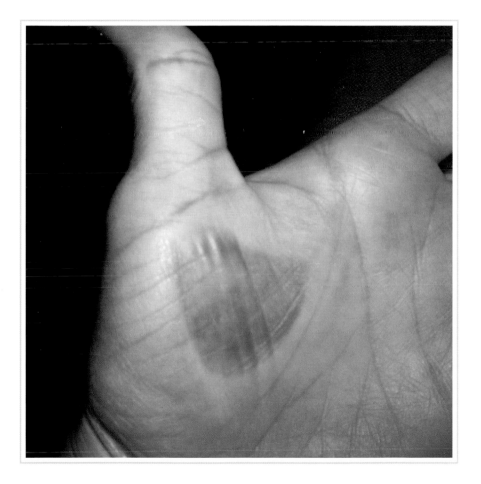

When you feel like you
have reached the end and
have nothing left to give,

I am here…

For love fills empty
spaces with life.

When you feel all alone,

I am here…

For love walks in the door,
even when everyone else
has walked out.

When you are broken,

I am here...

For love restores and
smoothes out the rough edges.

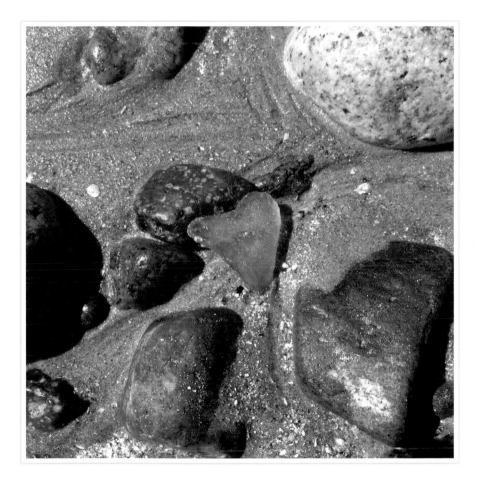

When you face oceans of
grief and disappointment,

I am here...

For love comforts and stays
close to the brokenhearted.

When you mess up and
fail time and again,

I am here…

For love forgives and
wipes the slate clean.

When you go through
fires of testing,

I am here…

For love comes to the rescue
and binds up wounds.

When the road makes you weary
and the luster starts to fade,

I am here...

For love makes the journey vibrant
and gives strength to endure.

When you are at a crossroads
and don't know where to turn,

I am here...

For love helps light the way
when the path is unclear.

When you wake up and feel blue,

I am here…

For love sticks through
thick and thin.

When you feel trapped,
as if there's no way out,

I am here…

For love carves out a way
through the seemingly impossible.

When you feel ugly
and unloveable,

I am here…

For love sees beauty in imperfection.

When your fears take over and
you want to hide in the darkness,

I am here...

For love drives fear into the ground.

When you are crushed and want to throw it all away,

I am here…

For love listens and
helps sort it all out.

When you go out on a limb
and make the wrong choice,

I am here…

For love won't let you fall
too deeply into the cracks.

When you need to pour
your thoughts on the table,

I am here…

For love is a sounding board
and does not spread judgment.

When your dreams don't line up,

I am here...

For love helps pave a new
road in the journey.

When you are stressed
and in the weeds,

I am here…

For love eases the burden
and refreshes the soul.

When you sink into
a deep, dark hole,

I am here...

For love reaches down with hope.

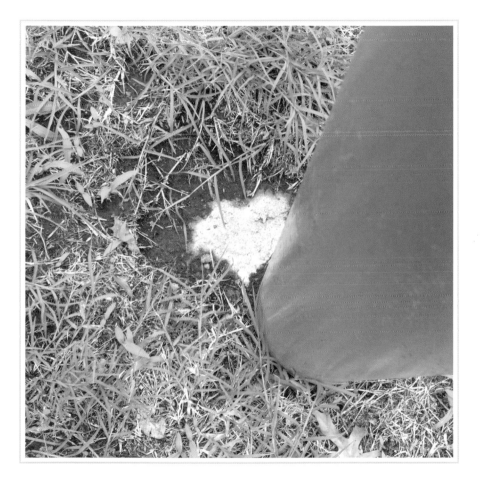

When you are misunderstood
and painted with disgrace,

I am here…

For love is compassionate
and will carry the sorrow.

When the sands are running out
and the end is drawing near,

I am here…

For love is like a rock
that cannot be moved.

Believe.

Trust.

Persevere.

Nothing will ever separate
you from my love.

For I am yours...

And you are mine.

never lose *heart*

The Lord your God is in your midst, a mighty one who will save; He will rejoice over you with gladness; He will quiet you by His love; He will exult over you with singing.

Zephaniah 3:17 (NIV)

about the author

Connie Smith grew up in Nashville, Tennessee. She graduated from the University of Tennessee in 1994 with a degree in Marketing and has spent most of her professional career in Nashville in the healthcare and publishing industries. After resigning as an executive in 2009 to pursue a business venture that did not unfold as she had hoped, she suddenly found herself lost and uninspired. In part, this began a quest to connect with God in a deeper way and, ultimately, to find her purpose. Little did she know the journey itself would produce the elements for a project she would later discover to be her sought-after passion. *Never Lose Heart* was born out of this journey and marks her debut as an inspirational writer. Along with her new-found love of writing, she enjoys spending time with family and friends, leading Bible study discussion groups at her home, cooking and entertaining, hiking, nature, and being outdoors.

share your photos

We would love for you to share your heart photos with us! Please email them to connie@neverloseheart.com along with your permission to include them in *Never Lose Heart's* Community Gallery at www.neverloseheart.com. We love to share the love!

To receive information about *Never Lose Heart* book signing events, special promotions, and new products/book projects, please sign up for our newsletter at www.neverloseheart.com.

And, please connect with us on Facebook and Instagram (neverloseheartbook) where we love to share encounters with God's love and inspirational messages that offer hope, comfort, and encouragement.